MULTICENE

Versions of poems have appeared in Nat Brut, Prolit,
Warm Milk Vol. 4, Ursus Americanus, as well as the
anthologies *Works & Days #2* published by beautiful day press
& *Anthropoetics* published by Violet Indigo Blue, Etc.
"The Weather" was produced as a digital chapbook by
rot house press. Thank you to the editors who generously
gave many of these poems their first appearances.

I am in constant debt and gratitude to my mom, dad,
and brother. I couldn't have written this book without
the love and support of Liz Janoff. And to the friends and
poets who read and encouraged these poems,
thank you all. I also want to thank Arteidolia Press,
who kindly agreed to give this book life.

ARTEIDOLIA PRESS
New York

arteidolia.com/arteidolia-press

First Edition
Library of Congress Control Number: 2023915269
ISBN: 979-8-9889702-0-0

MULTICENE

Nicodemus Nicoludis

arte povera press

New York

Planet, Earth, World

Planet, Earth, World

"...Then we go on, the world
always goes on, breaking us with its changes
until our form, exhausted, runs true."

Joanne Kyger

"Beloved,
I have to adore the earth."

Henry Dumas

In a moment

I am dressed up
like a poet
     And I am dreaming
     of staying awake
     for days to work
     on memory—
making maps of forests—
performing brute labor
in the underbrush
Atmospheric
     the flower fields
     slant up
     slightly coasting across
     an evening sky
     a fictitious wobbling
of tectonic plates and
granite boulders
It is uneasy, moving
underwater this way
I call out—Virgil—
can I plough
your fields?
Perform a poem
     in perfect rhythm
     behind a goat
     or sheep
     lounging in the afterglow
     of my own selfish

creation—
I understand
his hesitancy
to reveal the secret
of pastoral laziness
Soon I will find
the time
        to really look
        at mirrors
        I think
        they call that
scrying   concentrating
on the dying
ethereal   the total
weight of
just what
so far
has been lost
        Now I am growing
        my capacity for
        transformation—
I feel the thrust
of importance
but here I am
with a computer
hoping
        it'll take me
        somewhere

2

farther than god
or Congress
Is mysticism
the belief in
our own capacity
for change—
how do we know
how much other
people think
about us or
each other?

Where is the middle
in the theory
of middle
the passageway
to getting into
the underground
of my
or your heart?
I read
about Enlightenment
and wanted
to flog the modernity
out of me—
lash every
gestic impulse out—
revert to a

little frog—
a little drop of water
feeding a plant
hiding in the desert
        Shouldn't we all
        want to halve
        everything—
call the world
our semi-globe?

When spring begins,
we bring in
Abundance—
we guide
the stream
        downhill in
        expectation
        of falling water
twice-washing
the spittle plains
I call out
to Hilda—
        find god
        is lush
        nourishment—
        the sooty soil
        springing
        forward

with crocus

We will pray now

Lay down

our bodies

heavy in

endless toil

Endless capacity
for the plastic world
      My lungs heave
      in and out
      on the dance floor
and I'm
thinking about
calling in sick
to work
      for the rest
      of the week
Then I can
really get
to the pit
of it
      The hapless feeling
      of closing

your hands
and eyes
and looking
for light

The time to brave the sea—
The time to brave the unfaithful sea—
The time to brave the unfaithful sea and the setting stars

marking the lowest horizon,
the strap of shipping lanes
holding the Great Atlantic
sargassum belt—
When it rains
I will stay indoors
all day
conserving what
little output I spew
for the humble saints
of quiet comforts—

linoleum—clean sheets—delivery food—a white
candle from the grocery store—e-tip gloves—high
capacity magazines—battery packs—etc

Being born
we were
coughed up into circulation

Beginning each day
all my language
comes crusading
      back into my throat—
      eyeing the eye between
      here and the never-wild—
a poultice of finely
mixed solace
of dry meadows
      blooming nowtopias
      spontaneously grafting
      free will onto
      the side of a highway
      cloverleaf
 We must tell the truth that
not everything can grow in every place
Hold the very power
of the wooded seascape
      the dunes that curling up
      toward the houses
      perched closer
to the aluminum tide
lunar sparkling
ax-like over waves
crests pumping
toward shore—
      the memory of god is found in seaberries
      and I hear in the midnight wind a rustling

for the heavenly substance of moonlight

The whole world is becoming
like the bottom of the ocean
full and living
     in the satisfaction
     of existing

      Little worms borrowing down into the sand
      —a whale carcass feast—a pitch-black serenade
      of harmonious communion— The vision skews,
      a volcanic vent erupts—the shrimp and mussels
      laugh in the ripple-stillness consuming all sides
      of our political alignments—the crabs don't care
      about work so why do you?

I ask this landscape

for inspiration
       wanting to own
the monuments

              of deep time

      Not so much the past
but the abstracted   present forming
      and reforming
sediment in
         arkose breccia
                 like my body
      bending always
        to pick up napkins
     that have blown
       from the table
     to the sidewalk

Or like the red-tailed
           hawks perched
     across the street
          straining against
     the wind
       to dive and hunt
the pigeons and sparrows   kicking dirt
     or picking up

     small sticks carrying
them off somewhere
     unseen to me now
though I look intently

I just   want to know

where all this stuff   goes at the end
     of the day

But that is
my selfishness
     again always
     my daily habit
of confusing
the ocean floor
     for poetry

Or toxic clouds
flared in the Gulf
     as lightning or   campfires

For now
I am captured
by the

enormous stillness of old trees

and all the places

that still need to be
set on fire too

Winter this year

will come on slowly
over months
and I will continue
to feed on peonies
and the incomplete
universe working constantly
to unfinish itself

Estranged as I am

from hollowed mountains // clear cut and dynamited // running out of room // to further contort // like coral looking // for breath between // the statues swinging // in the midnight of // The Nation // Of course // I want hollow out // the sunset // swallow the midnight // light pollution

Do you ever think // we'll see between // the lattice of satellites // and 747s?

Of the fog

wrapped lazy around the ships mooring
        offshore distant but visibly mountainous
Juxtaposing lightly in the breeze
        the gulls gliding sunward and I
                                in my innocence
heap days onto the fire of human callow

Walking to the deli wanting coffee
        in the morning for breakfast
before the rest of the day
        this un-karmic circle
My sutric I scans the horizon
                the clouds
        the deoxidized reef
for the pose of god when he cast down
        the tsunami and/or hurricane

And for my mother again making dinner
        A place none of us will go back to

The rolling valley
The humble rock face
acned time in ribbons
blazed for this posterity of
drivel

after Allen Ginsberg

13

Do you really believe

animals
>   as we are
the terrain
>   of this life
out here
>   in the cold city

>   as we are
grasping for houses
>   and clean water
that in this heart
>   made from creatures
of long history
>   and ancient lava flows
there is space
>   for a new world
to grow out?

Lichen-black
>   the future is
the landlord
>   of today and so
the totality
>   of seashells created
in layers
>   all the beachfront
property will soon
>   be upturned

reclaimed
     And shameful
as we are
     we will mourn
the house and
     not the sand
The Nation
     and not
the grasses
     nor the exasperated
mountain brush

I am no longer surprised

by the places // we have // or will // have destroyed // by
tomorrow // morning

Time or // the future // works that way

Even now // as you // read this // somewhere // in the
world // something // is dying

How do you feel // about that?

Suddenly

I am again walking to the
apple orchard on the other side

of the woods behind my
parents' house under maple

and eastern redcedars paper birch
and various firs This story gets

simplified into energy time Or
the millions of years it took

to create the job
the loan
the banking collapse
the water cycle
the bunker buster

My generation is dying and so
are all the rest under the sun

in the arbitrary location of all
this violence we call

The Nation

I am jealous of the way a branch

breaks burdened with snow

under the fulling moon
tragic and languid

This isn't really the language of
disaster   touching though it may be

I am sorry for this sentiment
This cowardly retreat to the romance

of words while nearly all
my friends   like me   are waiting

for the future to happen
for The Nation to split open and rot

It would be nice to hear
the way those twigs would break

under my feet again To feel
the weight of apples

in my backpack watching the smoke
line from the chimney

plotting my course home

I hold in my hands

only a small area

      of the world from

           time to time
making my presence known
from the light I produce

      The dollars I spend on rent
      each month

Somewhere someone is burning
      toast and I

         am wasting
     as much time
as I can at work

           because even if art
       isn't protest I'll
         keep these poems
    close to me
     for the moment

We were all born into this balance of circles
       and delta mouths
so tender between meals and floods

How does

                      the poem
      form from
catastrophe and wind?

And how did we lose
      the presence of trees
         and the pure
             community of tundra days?

Our little regions

      not The Nation's exactly

      but tiny biorealms
         wooded and historical
      for a time

Now civilized   and propertied

Every night
      the Earth
rewrites this poem

The lacunae
      of bugs

sets in over the forests

And I am bed
                listening to my neighbor

idle his car

I disobey

the wind
      when examining
this interglacial verse
      and the way
      I am
in truth
      so human
set to hum
      my palinodes
like a riverbed
                Gigantic

      I am not going
to call this
      resistance
but maybe the actual
      slipping into
darkness like

      the cigarettes
      the men outside
      the deli smoke
between pulls
      from a bottle
of mamajuana

But I am only just
reading into this
        radiance as the
defiant soliloquy
        made exactly
as it should be
        alone and quite
lasting only
        for the last of us
who will cash our
        paychecks for
a view of the
        stars uncostly
and
        totalitarian

I forgot the time

I needed to be at work
while making coffee

It's early enough
to know that without asking

the Earth keeps breaking
into smaller parts

I name the morning
consumption

Or the unbearable call
to be productive

I just want to think about
us in bed as we roll closer
into each other
and I see the scar

on my knee from falling
on rocks at the beach
trying to be brave
for my brother

as he walked the tide pools
for the first time
after moving

from Pittsburgh to New Hampshire

Was the sand always
this purposeful?

We never found a lobster
Never understood how lungs work

Do
        we just
                keep going?
Should
        I keep
                going?

I don't think that's philosophy
Can I slow down for a moment now?

See life for its exchanges
The fission of wage-time
                free-time
                time-to-destination
                labor-time
        divided by
                value-time

We get closer to a revolution

when we start thinking

about time as pleasure
not commodity   Its value

a temporal ghost haunting
life until we stop time as material

//

In the
time
it takes
for you
to read
this poem
I will
have made
approximately
$ .50

I will not buy

a new palm plant
        when this one dies
Instead I will inhabit
        the stasis of its dying
and of my purchasing
        many different plants
I water as often
        as I remember
Remember I am not
        as caring as
I'd like to be
        about my habitat
in the city or
        in this atmosphere
of the hazed
        insurrection
of the concrete folded
        to make way
for new grass
                growing
                or overgrowing
is a form of
        perspective

        My language is
inadequate to describe
        the massive landscapes
I've driven through

smoking cigarettes

trying to get from here
        to there as many
of us are

Tomorrow
        I hope the morning
sun angles just right
        for us to lay down
in before work

        Our moment
of meditation on
        all that grows
and wilts
        grows again
and turns
        each captive flower
into a pipe bomb

Do you know when in despair

you lie down // day-blind // as the world at rest // waiting
for grief // like water // only growing // in the afternoon //
I am without // forethought mostly // and I am skeptical //
of ambition or // people with quotes // in the email
signatures

Does a seed try // to open or // does it // like a wave //
flex and heave // with the throb // of the center of
matter // infinite and fizzy // Don't you agree // it makes
sense // that the new // kind of money // is as
destructive // as this one // That you // mine it too

Nothing exists // without extirpation // or exhaustion

I will lie down // again in my grief // for stars and // other
small bodies // at peace with the light // as such // or the
celosia // in my mother's garden // growing for a time

A question arises

from the small beasts living their wilde fauna time
out of sight
                        thank god
of me
looking tho gently
for the next hillside view of the city

            Yes I have mellowed
my anxieties for
the moment sulking and spreading
lightly my arms
                        around the upturned
            oak trees killed
                        in a storm I spent
the morning waiting for in my apartment
wondering how safe
            I actually am from the effects of
corporations or seed patents

When this is all over
            meaning when
the days soften in contrast to the walls
bordering migration routes
            in contrast to the novel ruins
constructed from red wood ash
snowing softly over San Francisco
the fog burnished and burned
            know that

we could never take enough

to take back the glacier I saw
on vacation with my family
in Alaska that is
                        no longer there

Checking for rain

in the morning from bed
looking slowly from the curtains

to the street at the garbage truck

The men in orange and neon yellow
heaving bags into the mouth of the truck

as it wails and cries And I am
here thinking about the flooding

in Karachi   The worst ever
recorded in history — 134 dead

The water is still rising
around stores and apartments

My dad called me yesterday
to tell me that oil stocks

are rising again so I
make the motoring of cars

in the street the symbolic
center of this universe

My memory of the bay
I sat by watching boats

In and out under the bridge
Blue and white the ice

formed on the river
Remember snow?

The exhaustion of winter?

Erosion takes time

and in this blue light   I watch the sand
          marginally entering   in and out
of the ocean   from the blanket   with friends
drinking beer   and frozen margaritas
Time is made

of this kind   of afternoon quickness
          tenderly passing   along this moment
and that one the way ants
                              or bees
discard their dead   which in turn   turns to
mushrooms
          or other kinds of detritus

Or rather the   necrophoresis
          of next year's   lady slippers
or fiddle heads

after Jorie Graham

In search of migrations

I am mindless   and only finding
        now that it is   late September
                and almost fall
                        the grey clouds oscillating
        in this light   over the bridge   and buildings

I will write this eclogue
waiting for Liz to come home from work while

I listen to the Grateful Dead   "So Many Roads"
                                        "Candyman"
        at my desk   It turns out
        you can only mourn
the sunset so long before
        the poem becomes
                    more smoke
        or an opaque veil   jittering and placid
like nothingness
                or hands buried   in sand cool and
        protected for now

The tide is coming meaning
        these words
nice as they are   are fading fast
Like a caribou
        on the mountainside
in search of footing
I too stumble often

The lake isn't a lyric

or a body   It isn't
        my memory or a mirror
for the rotten and cliched moon
        half slanted and slanderous
There is just too much space
        in the fields
Deer and wildflowers have died
        all because of me
and my taking mouth
        asking always just please
one more night of drinking
        and cigarettes before CAPITAL
collapses this poem in on itself
        Patience is a luxury
as I lay further into
        northern New Hampshire
wealthy and wooded
        Once mostly farm fields
now new growth forest
and abandoned lumber mills
turned townhouses
I don't
        want to go
                to space Liz says
Neither do I

Is it the mania of owning

things or writing // in my notebook // bringing the //
streets or sunset // back from their // emptiness of
rhythm or // meanings // in the confusing // loneliness of
the afternoon // under some honey locust // wide and
flaying // ever outward

and I // lost in its totality

Is this the planet // the earth or the world // I am resting
and writhing on // in my small existence

It will be microplastic // that kills us // and it is very
important // for you to know // that right now // we did
not choose // this tree or / who planted it // We did not
kill this world // but watched // it be killed // by a planet
of ownership // by those who // did the choosing //
first // The mapping and probing first

There is no perfection

in the world outside the red
of a cardinal's wing
or the way my grandmother picked
roses anytime we visited
making sure the thorns
were broken and discarded

I wish
I cared
for the
whole Earth
this way

Thoughtful and delicate cooing on
a riverbank like Liz in bed
in the spring holding
on to the spinning city
clenching itself into a vortex
or an endless gyration
of minerals and granite
the soft bedrock of Manhattan
mostly bones and swamp
we almost forget
the amount of people   killed
      captured
         and held
here

Even the poppies
growing under the subway tracks
between the MTA workers' cars
find something worth living for
if only to produce more living
more orange for a season
or an evening
like a full moon birthing
itself from nothingness
from space
from the conditional weight
between the peace of the wild
and the accumulation needed
to condition me to use paper towels
and plastic sandwich baggies

All I want

is boundless Earth // I am the least // difficult man // in
that way // Lying prostrated // the grasses are // talking //
to me again explaining // the cycle of food // the history
of guano // mines in South America // the commodification //
of shit

The sky is vague

Blue like the wing // of a seagull stroked // at a great
distance // so in squinting // I am still trying // to
understand // the humility // that comes with touch // just
this simple expression // of green of leaves etc

Everywhere // the pastoral // easily beautiful // but
nowhere is the pasture // Until I fall to the Earth
// I will not move

after Frank O'Hara

It is very dangerous

to forget   the forest and fields
are boring
                mono-monotonous
and humdrum

Oh please no more corn or lawns
                I am done   dreaming of tomorrow
        we must accept   that parts of the Amazon
will never come back

Strip-mined
                open-pitted
                                spilt
        and burned

I will never care about a millionaire
or Kentucky bluegrass

If this is a song
        I will only sing it
at midnight
        watching
the comet out the window
        the A/C cooling
the sweat
        from my stomach
and chest

The Weather

Regional Weather Roundup
National Weather Service New York NY
1100 AM EDT TUE AUG 01 2023

Note: **"FAIR"** indicates few or no clouds below 12,000 feet
with no
significant weather and/or obstructions to **visibility**.

NYZ071-072-176-178-NJZ106-104-011600-
New York City **Metro** Area

CITY	SKY/**WX**	TMP	**DP**	**RH**	WIND	**PRES**
REMARKS						
Central Park	SUNNY	75	47	36	NE9	30.17R
World Trd Ctr	NOT **AVBL**					
Bronx Lehman **C**	N/A	73	52	46	N8	N/A
LaGuardia Arpt	MOSUNNY	75	48	38	NE10	30.13S
Queens College	N/A	73	48	40	NE10	N/A
Kennedy Intl	MOSUNNY	76	49	38	NE12G21	30.14R
Breezy Point	N/A	73	N/A	N/A	NE10	N/A
Brooklyn Coll	N/A	73	46	38	N8	N/A
Staten Island	N/A	75	45	33	N8	N/A
Newark/Liberty	MOSUNNY	77	48	35	N9G18	30.14R
Teterboro	SUNNY	75	50	41	NE9	30.13R

Liz and her family have a group text about the weather.

Whenever my mom calls the first thing she asks about

is the weather.

She wants to know the difference

between Fort Worth's and New York's weather.

Before I go to bed

and when I first wake up

I check the weather.

In my hand

I hold the commodity

of weather.

Little graphs and radar

dance for me,

tracking bands

of clouds;

or, I watch a video on how spring rainfall rates

effect flooding

in the Great Plains;

 or, read more

on the improvements

they've made

on being able to track increasing

changes in the weather.

I deal with the ads

because I don't want to pay

to have a premium experience

with the weather.

I got into an argument with my cousin trying to explain

the difference between climate and weather.

We abstract our present,

split time and movement into forces

of nature and I want to measure

the distance of the future

in capsules of weather.

I wonder what Thoreau would think about today's weather.

Would he bask in it,

find god in it; or,

look across a wooded river

to find new euphemisms for a

denatured society in weather?

Birds and other animals move by the weather.

Whole colonies

triggered

by minute shifts in weather.

The rise and fall of pressure

thinning raindrops pulsing out weather.

Lay your head

on the pulse   of world   and feel   it pump

through weather.

Birds and geese come home earlier,

or later, if at all, because

of the changing

weather.

I had a panic attack and Liz said

it was because of the weather.

Our ancestors used to

pray to the weather.

"The higher

the clouds

the nicer

the weather."

Before you could hunt or sail,

you had to study patterns of weather.

Read the clouds

each night,

divine weather,

find them narrating

a long story

about the history

of society,

the building up of

instruments to follow the weather.

Looking to the stars

I hope they might show

what tomorrow

will bring

or if we might

have nice weather

Stories tell of

civilizations lost

because of the weather.

They raised their hands and heads,

turned towards god

or the sun

and he said, "Here,

take this weather."

When I drive my friend's car

or sit in a cab I can hear the Earth,

in the future saying, "Here,

take this weather."

The Weather Channel

spends tens of thousands

of dollars on "Altered Reality" CGI

videos so you can watch

the water rise around a reporter

as they give the facts

on levee tolerance to storm surge

or comparisons of snowmelt totals

flowing into the Mississippi

and other effects of extreme weather.

Going to work

gets more tedious

depending on the weather.

I want to ride my bike,

but first I'll check the weather.

Liz wanted to go to the beach,

but I said

"depending on the weather."

My dad says planes hardly ever crash

because of weather.

That most severe turbulence

comes from the wake

of other planes not from weather.

Or convection from

heated ground pushing air

towards the sky and

in the plane you feel

the cosmic rush and

the shifting winds forming

the weather.

"It's West Texas so you can never predict the weather."

My friend got Lyme disease

and he moved to Marfa for the weather.

My Yia Yia got sick

and moved to Fort Worth for the weather.

I had a friend who thought

the government controlled the weather.

He said that one day

they would kill people

using a machine

that made the weather.

I turn on the radio

to listen to the weather.

Everyday we

hear a new report of

weather, feel the

weather, talk about

various ups and downs in

temperature and humidity,

between friends and family,

all us conversing

over weather.

Now I think and write

and read about the weather.

Read Lucretius

and think about atoms of weather

Weather and weather.

Weather moving into

other weathers,

shaping a totality of weather.

All the atoms of the world

collide and press together

forging a global body of weather.

The material of weather,

like plates of shale exposed to air

for the first time in millennium

lining the sides of a coal mine

in rural Kentucky,

we are layering

our grief and consumption

into stratospheres of weather.

Now, we write poems on the weather

without knowing they're

about the weather.

And we have conversations

about the weather

across the world;

about the first hurricane of the season,

what it might be named,

always us wanting

to see ourselves and

all the matter we've (re)made

and thought of

in the weather.

In the future

our relationship to power

and the Earth will fundamentally

change because of the weather.

Do you get sad

by just looking at

the weather?

Each thunderstorm or lack of thunderstorm,

each snowfall or lack of snowfall,

gloss as symptoms of the dying world,

the world in catastrophe humming out

morbid centos in patterns of weather.

This is a poem about money and the weather.

Capital and the weather.

Wealth and the weather.

Exploitation and the weather.

The world and the weather.

Migration and the weather.

The plastic ocean and the weather.

Everyone everywhere

crying out for

relief and revolution

in the midnight of the weather.

Notes

"I ask this landscape"

Wendell Berry's poems were a great inspiration for this, and many other poems, and the line "enormous stillness of old trees" is from his poem "History."

"Of the fog"

Allen Ginsburg appeared on William F. Buckley's *Firing Line* on May 7, 1968 and read the poem "Wales Visitation." The composition of this poem follows his and was written with his voice and cadence in mind.

"Erosion takes time"

The thematic of the poem is inspired by and uses the line "in this blue light" from Jorie Graham's "San Sepolcro."

"All I want"

The title of the poem comes from Frank O'Hara's "Meditations in an Emergency" and rearranges language and images from the poem.

www.ingramcontent.com/pod-product-compliance
Lightning Source LLC
LaVergne TN
LVHW041308080426
835510LV00009B/903